D0871780

Save Wisely

BY HEATHER E. SCHWARTZ

amicus
high interest

Amicus High Interest is published by Amicus
P.O. Box 1329, Mankato, MN 56002
www.amicuspublishing.us

Library of Congress Cataloging-in-Publication Data
Schwartz, Heather E.
 Save wisely / by Heather E. Schwartz.
     pages cm. – (Money smarts)
Includes bibliographical references and index.
Audience: K to Grade 3.
Summary: "This photo-illustrated book for elementary readers
describes the benefits of saving money that is earned or
received. Gives tips on saving for big and small purchases and
how banks can help keep money safe"– Provided by publisher.
ISBN 978-1-60753-794-6 (library binding)
ISBN 978-1-60753-903-2 (ebook)
1. Savings accounts–Juvenile literature. 2. Finance, Personal–
Juvenile literature. 3. Money–Juvenile literature. I. Title.
 HG1660.A3S384 2015
 332.1'752–dc23

                              2014036517

Editor: Wendy Dieker
Series Designer: Kathleen Petelinsek
Book Designer: Aubrey Harper
Photo Researcher: Derek Brown

Photo Credits: 237/Paul Bradbury/Ocean/Corbis cover; Don
Bayley/Getty 5; Hero Images Inc./Corbis 6-7; Hero Images/
Getty 9; Marc Debnam/Getty 10; Keith Leuit/Design Pics/
Corbis 13; Steven Errico/Getty 14; 13/Matthias Tunger/
Digital Vision/Ocean/Corbis 17; michaeljung/Shutterstock
18; Laura Doss/Corbis 21; DreamPictures/Getty 22; 2/Ryan
McVay/Ocean/Corbis 24-25; Jamie Grill/Getty 26; Jose Luis
Pelaez Inc/Getty 29

Printed in Malaysia.

10 9 8 7 6 5 4 3 2 1

Table of Contents

Your Money, Your Decisions

Have you ever wanted something very **expensive**? Big stuff like computers, bikes, and smartphones cost a lot of money. How could you ever **afford** something like that? You don't have enough money! The answer is simple. Save up money first.

Tablets are expensive.
You'll have to save up your
money to buy one.

Saving money starts with getting it. Maybe you earn money. You might do chores at home. You might work for neighbors. You might sell things at your family's garage sale. Maybe you get money as gifts, too. Relatives might send money on your birthday.

Do you earn money by helping do yard work?

When you have money, you have a choice to make. Do you want to spend it? Or do you want to save it? If you spend it right away, you could buy something small. You might get a treat from the ice cream truck, for example. If you save it, you could buy something more expensive later.

 What if I can't stop myself from spending?

You could choose to buy ice cream treats with your money.

 You don't have to save every penny you get. When you have money, divide it up. Save some. Spend the rest.

Making sure your money is safe is an important step in saving.

Keeping Cash Safe

Money is **valuable**. Always keep it someplace safe. At home, you could put it in a piggy bank, a jar, or an envelope. Make sure pets can't reach it. They might chew bills. Make sure younger siblings won't find it. They might think it's theirs to take. You can't always get lost cash back. Keep track of it!

The bank is another place to store your money. You could open a **savings account**. Money is safe in a savings account. It can't be lost. It can't be destroyed. If it is stolen, the bank will replace it. Ask your parents about opening a savings account if you don't have one.

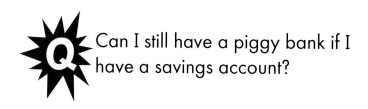
Q Can I still have a piggy bank if I have a savings account?

Putting money in the bank is one of the best ways to save.

 Yes! You can save up your coins at home. When your piggy bank is full, you can take it to the bank.

Bring your cash to the bank.
The interest earned on your
cash adds up over time.

Another good thing about banks is that they pay **interest**. That means the bank pays you to keep your money there. The interest is added to your account. Interest isn't a lot of money. Suppose you have $100 in your account. You might earn 50 cents interest in one year. Still, it's free money. And it can add up over time.

Saving for the Short-Term

Suppose you're saving for a new computer game. You want it fast, right? But it costs $30. You need to build your **short-term savings**. That way, you can buy the game while you're still a kid. It does take time to build short-term savings though. Suppose you earn $10 a month. If you save it all, you will have $30 in three months.

Use short-term savings to buy
things that don't cost very much.

Deciding which things
you really want to buy or
save for can be tough.

 Q Why do I want so many things
I see in TV commercials?

While you're saving money, it's tempting to spend it. Imagine your savings goal is $50. You've saved $30. Then you see a $15 toy you'd like to buy. You could spend the money. You could get the toy. But then you will only have $15 left. It will take longer to reach your savings goal.

 Companies work to make their products look really cool. They want you to buy their products. That's how they make money.

Saving money isn't always easy. It takes **self-control**. You have to choose not to spend. It takes dedication. You have to focus on your savings goal. If you keep saving, you'll reach that goal. You'll have the money you need to buy something you really want.

 What if saving takes so long, I don't want what I've saved for anymore?

If you keep saving, you will be able to buy what you want.

 Then you're ahead of the game! You can plan a different purchase with plenty of money ready to spend.

You'll need to save for a long
time to be able to buy a car.

Saving for the Future

What if you want to save for college? Or for a car? Those things are very expensive. And you don't need the money until you are older. For those purchases, you need to build **long-term savings**. It takes a long time to build long-term savings. But you have years to do it.

Your long-term savings are safest in the bank. Over time, you can add money to the account. And the bank will add interest. It will grow over the years. When your money is in the bank, it will be out of sight. You won't be so tempted to spend it.

A banker helps add money to your account.

It is wise to start saving
for things you'll buy when
you are a grown-up.

Q Can't I just get **loans** from the bank when I grow up?

You might be a teenager when you spend your long-term savings. You might be an adult. You might even save until you are a grandparent! It may seem silly to plan so far ahead. But saving now will help you in the future. You won't have to worry. You'll have the money you need.

Maybe. But the problem with loans is that banks charge interest. You have to pay back more than you borrowed! It's wiser to save money to buy things.

Don't Quit! Save!

Saving is the solution when you want something you can't afford. You might not get what you want right away. You just have to keep saving. Stay focused. Don't give up. You can reach your goal. What will you save money for?

It took time, but this girl saved
a bunch of coins. What do
you think she's saving for?

Glossary

afford To have enough money to buy something.

expensive To cost a lot of money.

interest A small bit of money the bank pays you for saving money in an account; also a small bit of money a customer has to pay on a loan.

loan An agreement with a bank to borrow money to buy something expensive.

long-term savings Money that is set aside to be used many years from now.

savings account An arrangement with the bank for them to keep your money safe.

self-control To keep doing something you want to do; or to not do something really tempting.

short-term savings Money that is saved to buy something in a short time; a few weeks or months is short-term.

valuable Something has great worth.

Read More

Bateman, Katherine R. *The Young Investor: Projects and Activities for Making Your Money Grow.* Chicago: Chicago Review Press, 2010.

Hansen, Mark Victor. *The Richest Kids In America.* East Brunswick, New Jersey: Hansen House Publishing, 2009.

Larlitz, Gail and Debbie Honig. *Growing Money: A Complete Investing Guide for Kids.* New York: Price Stern Sloan, 2010.

Websites

The Great Piggy Bank Adventure
piggybank.disney.go.com

The Mint: Saving Calculator
www.themint.org/kids/saving-calculator.html

**PBS Kids: It's My Life:
Money: Managing My Money**
pbskids.org/itsmylife/money/managing/article8.html

Index

About the Author

Heather E. Schwartz has written books for young readers on all kinds of topics. She was excited to write about money because it can be earned and used in so many interesting ways. She recently spent some savings on a fun purchase: two kittens! Visit Heather's website at www.heathereschwartz.com.